INTRODUCTIC

CW01508677

Welcome to the world of dinosaurs! In this magical land, where towering trees and vibrant plains stretch as far as the eye can see, a group of young dinosaurs embark on thrilling adventures. Each dinosaur has its own special home and a heart full of curiosity, ready to discover the wonders of its prehistoric world.

Meet Milo, a curious T-Rex who loves to follow mysterious tracks through the jungle. Trixie, a playful Triceratops, enjoys exploring bright, flower-filled meadows. Stella, the adventurous Stegosaurus, is always eager to uncover hidden valleys and secret treasures.

In this enchanting collection, your little ones will join these dinosaur friends on exciting journeys, where they'll face new challenges, learn valuable lessons, and discover the true meaning of courage, kindness, and friendship.

"5-Minute Bedtime Stories: Dinosaurs" is the perfect read for parents and children alike – a delightful way to inspire young minds, spark their imagination, and end the day with a smile. Perfect for little explorers who are ready to dream big!

Tamba's Big Heart

TAMBA, THE SPECIAL T-REX

Once upon a time, a young T-Rex named Tamba lived in a land of rolling green hills and a bright blue sky.

Now, Tamba was a very special T-Rex. His golden-red fringes shimmered in the sunlight, making him more dazzling than anyone else in the valley of dinosaurs. But these beautiful fringes also made him different; sometimes, different can feel lonely.

Tamba loved exploring and meeting new friends. However, no matter how friendly he was, the other dinosaurs always seemed unsure about playing with him. The thought of having fun with future friends made him hopeful every day, but sometimes it ended with Tamba walking back home alone, watching the sun dip below the hills.

A WISH FOR FRIENDSHIP

One sunny morning, Tamba was wandering through the lush, green forest, his tail swishing happily behind him. He heard giggles and laughter drifting through the trees.

Guided by the joyful sounds, he soon stumbled upon a group of Triceratops, their horns glistening, as they chased fluttering butterflies in the warm, gentle breeze.

"Can I play too?" Tamba asked, his eyes sparkling with anticipation.

The Triceratops stopped their game, exchanging nervous glances.

The Triceratops stopped their game, exchanging nervous glances.

"Hmm... well..." one of them mumbled, shuffling its feet.

"You might be too big," said another hesitantly.

"And... hmm... what if you play too rough? We bruise easily. "

Tamba's heart sank like a stone in a pond, but he didn't let the feeling show. He painted a brave smile on his face.

"That's okay. Maybe another time!" he chirped, though his voice was softer now.

As he wandered away, Tamba decided to explore the forest's edge, where the trees were older, and the air was filled with the songs of chirping birds. Tamba loved discovering its secrets in the forest was a place of mystery and wonder.

THE CRY FOR HELP

Later that day, as the sun began its descent, painting the sky in hues of pink and orange, Tamba heard frightened cries coming from nearby.

His ears perked up, and his heart hoped it was a call for help he could answer.

Following the sounds, he soon came upon a fearsome sight: a pack of Velociraptors, six in number, circling a group of terrified dinosaurs—a gentle Brachiosaurus, the

timid Stegosaurus, and several Triceratops who had been chasing butterflies earlier that day.

"Stay back!" growled the biggest Velociraptor, flashing its razor-sharp teeth, each tooth glinting menacingly.

The Brachiosaurus trembled, its long neck shivering like a leaf.

The Stegosaurus, always gentle, huddled with its friends, trying to make itself as small as possible.

The Triceratops that Tamba had met earlier whimpered, their courage wilting under the Velociraptors' fierce gaze.

THE ROAR OF COURAGE

In that critical moment, Tamba felt his heart pounding in his chest, each beat as loud as a drum.

But as fear crept up his spine, a new feeling rushed through him—courage, strong and bright, like the rays of the morning sun.

Tamba stepped forward, his mighty feet thumping against the ground. The earth shook with each step he took.

He puffed out his chest, and with a deep breath, he let out the loudest, mightiest roar he could muster.

The sound cracked through the forest like thunder, echoing through the trees, reaching every corner of the land.

The Velociraptors, startled by Tamba's thundering roar, paused.

Their leader blinked in surprise, and one by one, they backed away slowly.

They were not expecting such bravery from the young T-Rex.

With a final, hesitant look at Tamba's shimmering fringes, the Velociraptors turned tail and fled into the forest's depths.

A HERO AND A FRIEND

Cheers erupted among the rescued dinosaurs.

The Brachiosaurus lifted its head high in gratitude.

The Stegosaurus wagged its spiky tail happily, and the Triceratops danced around Tamba, their previous hesitancy forgotten.

"Thank you, Tamba!" said one of the Triceratops, its voice filled with admiration and joy. "You were so brave!"

"We were wrong about you," another added. "You're not just big, you're also kind and strong!"

From that day on, everyone wanted to be Tamba's friend.

His difference became his strength, and his shimmering gold-red fringes no longer set him apart but made him a beloved part of their community.

And so, in the land of rolling green hills and bright blue skies, Tamba the T-Rex lived happily ever after, always surrounded by friends and adventure.

Brave Triceratops and the Lost Egg

A KIND AND STRONG DINOSAUR

Once upon a time, in the heart of a lush, green valley, there lived a brave triceratops named Trixie. With her three magnificent horns and a frilled crown, Trixie was not only the strongest dinosaur in the valley but also the kindest. She spent her days exploring the vibrant forest, helping her friends, and playing hide-and-seek with the little dinosaur chicks.

A MYSTERIOUS DISCOVERY

One sunny morning, as Trixie wandered near the sparkling river, she stumbled upon a peculiar sight. A tiny, glimmering egg sat alone on a mossy rock. It was unlike any egg she had ever seen. It shimmered in shades of blue and gold, reflecting the sunlight most magically.

"Oh, my!" Trixie exclaimed, lowering her head to get a better look. "Who could have lost this egg?"

Just then, her friend Benny the little brontosaurus ambled over, his long neck stretching high above the trees.

"What do you have there, Trixie?" he asked, his eyes wide with curiosity.

"I found this beautiful egg, Benny! But it looks lost," Trixie replied. "We should find its owner."

With a determined nod, Trixie and Benny decided to embark on an adventure to reunite the egg with its mother.

SEEKING WISDOM

They knew that the forest was home to many creatures, so they began their search by visiting Mabel, the wise old pterodactyl, who lived high in the cliffs.

As they approached Mabel's nest, they called out, "Mabel! Mabel! Do you know who this egg belongs to?"

Mabel fluttered down, her feathers ruffling in the breeze. "Ah, what a lovely egg!

I believe it belongs to an oviraptor. They often lay their eggs near the river. You should check there!"

"Thank you, Mabel!" Trixie and Benny chimed, their hearts full of hope. They raced down the hill, eager to see if they could find the oviraptor.

The wind whooshed past them as they bounded through the tall grass, dodging ferns and leaping over fallen logs. The sound of rushing water grew louder with every step, guiding them toward the riverbank.

A LOST LITTLE OVIRAPTOR

When they reached the riverbank, they found a small clearing filled with colorful wildflowers. But there was no sign of the oviraptor. Just then, they spotted a fluffy little oviraptor, hopping around in circles, looking quite distressed.

"What's wrong, little one?" Trixie asked gently, crouching down to the oviraptor's level.

"I can't find my egg!" the little oviraptor cried, tears welling in her bright eyes. "I lost it while I was playing."

Trixie's heart sank. "Could it be this egg?" she asked, nudging the shimmering egg closer.

"Oh, yes! That's my egg!" the little oviraptor exclaimed, her face lighting up with joy. "Thank you so much for finding it!"

THE SHADOW OF DANGER

Just as the oviraptor reached for her egg, a shadow swooped overhead. It was a fierce-looking dinosaur, a hungry velociraptor, that had seen the commotion from a distance. "Well, well, what do we have here?" he sneered, his eyes glinting with mischief.

"A lovely little snack!"

Trixie's heart raced. She knew they had to protect the egg and the little oviraptor. With a deep breath, she stood tall and faced the velociraptor. "You will not take this egg!" she declared, her voice steady and strong.

Benny, standing beside her, gave a brave nod. "We're not afraid of you!" he added, lifting his tail to show he was ready to defend their new friend.

The velociraptor hesitated, eyeing the two brave dinosaurs. He was bigger, but he could see the determination in Trixie's eyes and the courage in Benny's stance.

"You think you can scare me off?"

he growled, but something in Trixie's fierce expression made him rethink.

After a tense moment, the velociraptor scoffed and turned away, deciding it was better to seek an easier meal elsewhere. "Fine! But don't think this is over!" he called as he scampered off into the forest.

A FRIENDSHIP SEALED WITH COURAGE

With the danger gone, Trixie, Benny, and the little oviraptor all breathed a sigh of relief. "You were so brave, Trixie!" the little oviraptor squeaked, hugging her egg close. "Thank you for protecting me!"

Trixie smiled, her heart swelling with pride. "We're all brave when we stick together," she said, nudging Benny affectionately.

From that day on, Trixie, Benny, and the little oviraptor became the best of friends. They played together, explored the forest, and shared many more adventures. And every time they saw the shimmering egg, they remembered that bravery comes in many forms, and together, they could face anything the valley threw at them.

THE LEGEND OF TRIXIE THE BRAVE

And so, the legend of Trixie the Brave Triceratops and the lost egg spread throughout the valley, inspiring all the little dinosaurs to be courageous and kind, just like Trixie. Whenever a challenge arose, they remembered her bravery and how one small dinosaur could make a big difference. Trixie's story became a shining example of kindness and courage that would be passed down for generations to come.

Stegosaurus and the Mystery of the Shiny Stone

THE FOREST OF WHIMSY

In a lush, vibrant land filled with towering trees and sparkling streams, there lived a friendly Stegosaurus named Stella. Stella was no ordinary dinosaur; she had a beautiful row of plates on her back that shimmered in the sunlight, just like the stars in the night sky. She loved to explore the Forest of Whimsy, where magical creatures danced and flowers sang sweet melodies. Every day was an adventure, but today was different.

THE DISCOVERY

As Stella wandered near the Rainbow River, she spotted something glimmering at the water's edge. With her curiosity piqued, she approached the shiny object, her heart fluttering with excitement. There, nestled between the pebbles, was the most extraordinary stone she had ever seen. It sparkled like a million fireflies trapped in a glass bubble.

"What a beautiful stone!" Stella exclaimed. But as she tried to pick it up with her big, clumsy feet, the stone rolled away, bouncing along the riverbank.

"Oh no!" Stella cried as she chased after it. The shiny stone danced just out of her reach, gleaming and gliding like a playful little fish.

THE QUEST BEGINS

Determined to catch the stone, Stella enlisted the help of her friends. First, she visited Benny the Bunny, who had big ears and even bigger ideas. "Benny, can you help me find the shiny stone?" she asked, her eyes sparkling with hope.

"Of course, Stella!" Benny replied, twitching his nose with excitement. "Let's gather our friends and solve the mystery together!"

They hopped over to find Lucy the Ladybug, who was busy lounging on a leaf, and Sam the Squirrel, who was expertly gathering acorns. Stella shared her discovery, and the group cheered with enthusiasm. Together, they formed a plan to catch the elusive shiny stone.

THE GREAT ADVENTURE

With Benny leading the way, they followed the trail of sparkling dust left behind by the stone. It led them through the forest, past the Singing Saplings and the Whispering Willows. The friends laughed and sang as they searched, their spirits high.

Suddenly, they came across a wise old Owl perched on a branch.

"Who, who goes there?" the Owl hooted, tilting his head curiously.

"It's us! We're on a quest to find a shiny stone!" Benny exclaimed.

The Owl's eyes widened with interest.

"A shiny stone, you say? I may know a thing or two. Follow the path of the glittering petals, and you shall find what you seek."

"Thank you, wise Owl!" Stella called as they hurried off, eager to follow the Owl's advice.

THE GLITTERING PETALS

As they continued their journey, they discovered a trail of petals that sparkled like diamonds. The friends marched bravely, guided by the shimmering path. Along the way, they encountered playful butterflies and giggling frogs, who all joined in their search for the mysterious stone.

After a while, they reached a clearing filled with twinkling flowers that lit up the area like a fairyland. And there, right in the center of the clearing, was the shiny stone! It glowed brighter than anything they had ever seen.

THE STONE'S SECRET

But just as they approached, the ground trembled, and a gentle voice echoed, "To claim the shiny stone, you must answer my riddle." It was the Guardian of the Stone, a magnificent creature made of soft, glowing light.

Stella and her friends nodded eagerly, ready for the challenge.

"What has keys but can't open locks? What has space but no room? What has places but no room?" the Guardian asked, smiling.

The friends huddled together, thinking hard. "I know!" Lucy shouted. "It's a piano!"

"Very clever," the Guardian said with a twinkle in his eye.

"You have proven yourselves worthy."

With a wave of his shimmering hand, the Guardian allowed them to take the stone. Stella carefully picked it up, and it felt warm and comforting in her hands.

A GIFT OF FRIENDSHIP

Stella looked at her friends, their eyes sparkling with joy.

"This stone is not just beautiful; it represents our adventure and friendship!" she declared.

Benny, Lucy, and Sam cheered. They decided to place the shiny stone in the heart of the forest, where everyone could see it and remember their special day together.

From that day on, the shiny stone became a symbol of their friendship, reminding all the creatures in the Forest of Whimsy that together, they could solve any mystery and embark on countless adventures.

As the seasons changed, the stone remained, its glow never fading, just like their bond.

And so, Stella the Stegosaurus and her friends continued to explore their magical world, creating memories that would shine as brightly as the stone they had discovered together.

Sometimes, new friends would gather around the stone, adding their own stories to its growing legend.

The Diplodocus Who Wanted to Reach the Stars

ONCE UPON A TIME IN DINOLAND

In the lush land of DinoLand, where lush green forests swayed and bubbling rivers flowed, lived a kind-hearted diplodocus named Daisy. Daisy was not an ordinary dinosaur. She was the tallest among her friends, with a neck that stretched high enough to tickle the soft, fluffy clouds. Yet Daisy had an extraordinary dream—she wanted to touch the stars.

THE DREAMER'S HEART

Every night, when the dinosaurs of DinoLand snuggled in their nests to sleep, Daisy would look up at the shimmering night sky. Stars gleamed like twinkling diamonds, and the moon smiled softly down at her. "Oh, how I wish I could touch the stars," Daisy would sigh with a hopeful heart.

Her friend, Timmy the Triceratops, would often say, "Daisy, stars are too far away! Even with your long neck, you can't reach them." But Daisy's dreams were bigger than the tallest trees or the highest mountains.

THE WISE OWL'S ADVICE

One day, while Daisy was nibbling on juicy leaves, she met Olly the Wise Owl. Olly was known across DinoLand for his wisdom and age-old stories. Daisy shared her dream with Olly, hoping he would know how to reach the stars.

"Dear Daisy," Olly hooted kindly, "stars are indeed very far. But dreams that seem unreachable are often the most precious. They guide your heart and inspire you to do great things."

Daisy listened carefully, her eyes filled with wonder. Olly continued, "Embrace your dreams, even if they seem impossible. Sometimes, the journey is just as beautiful as the destination."

THE PLAN AND THE CLIMB

Inspired by Olly's words, Daisy decided to try and get as close to the stars as she possibly could. She thought of the tallest hill in DinoLand, known as Star Peak. If she could climb it, maybe, just maybe, she'd be closer to the twinkling sky.

With determination in her heart, Daisy set off to climb Star Peak. Buster the brave Stegosaurus joined her, offering to carry supplies. Their friends cheered them on, waving leafy banners and singing happy songs.

THE JOURNEY OF FRIENDSHIP

As they climbed Star Peak, Daisy realized her dream wasn't just about touching stars. It was about the journey she was sharing with her friends. They laughed at funny-shaped clouds, played hide and seek behind rocks, and shared stories that made their hearts warm and fuzzy.

"It's amazing how dreams can bring friends together," Daisy thought with a smile.

ALMOST TOUCHING THE SKY

Finally, Daisy and Buster reached the top of Star Peak. They stood there, panting and giggling, as the sun began to set, painting the sky with shades of pink and orange. As night fell, the stars appeared, brighter and closer than ever before.

Daisy stretched her neck and stood tall. She couldn't touch the stars, but she felt their magic all around her. "Even if I can't touch them," she whispered, "I can always dream of them."

WISDOM OF THE STARS

As Daisy gazed at the stars, she remembered Olly's words about dreams guiding the heart. Right there, she realized that dreams were special, not because they were easy to reach, but because they filled her with happiness and wonder.

Sitting on Star Peak, surrounded by twinkling stars and dear friends, Daisy understood that her dream of reaching the

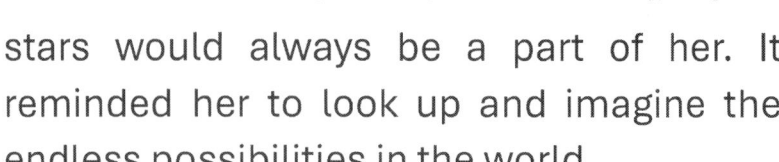

stars would always be a part of her. It reminded her to look up and imagine the endless possibilities in the world.

HAPPILY EVER AFTER

From that day on, Daisy no longer felt sad about not touching the stars. She knew dreams were like stars themselves—shining brightly and forever inspiring.

And so, Daisy the diplodocus, with her tall neck and big dreams, lived happily ever after in DinoLand, teaching her friends that no dream was too big if it could make their hearts glow as brightly as the starry sky.

DAISY'S DREAMS

And every night, as the stars sparkled in the sky, Daisy would wish upon them, dreaming of new adventures and endless possibilities in the magical world of DinoLand.

Her dreams, like the stars, seemed endless, and with each new day, she discovered even more ways to make the world a brighter place.

The Ankylosaurus and the Unexpected Friend

A QUIET MEADOW

Once upon a time, in a lush, green meadow where the sun shone bright and flowers bloomed in a rainbow of colors, lived a gentle giant named Aida the Ankylosaurus. Aida was a magnificent creature, covered in bumpy armor and equipped with a spiky tail. She was known for her strength and kind heart, but she often felt lonely in her big world.

A LONELY LIFE

Every day, Aida watched as other dinosaurs played together. The swift Velociraptors raced through the trees, while the graceful Pterodactyls soared high above the clouds. Aida wished she could join in the fun, but her heavy body made it hard for her to keep up. So, she would settle down by the river, munching on tasty plants, dreaming of friendship.

A SURPRISE ENCOUNTER

One sunny afternoon, while Aida was enjoying her lunch, she heard a strange sound. It was a soft whimpering noise coming from behind a bush. Curious, Aida carefully waddled over to see what it was. Peeking through the leaves, she spotted a tiny creature with big, round eyes and fluffy fur.

"Hello there!" Aida said softly. "What's wrong?"

The little creature looked up, trembling with fear. "I'm Benny the Bunny," he squeaked. "I got lost while hopping around, and now I can't find my way home!"

AIDA TO THE RESCUE

Aida's heart melted at the sight of Benny. "Don't worry, Benny! I can help you find your home. Climb up on my back, and I'll take you wherever you need to go!"

Benny's eyes widened in surprise. "You would do that for me?"

"Of course!" Aida replied with a warm smile. Benny hopped onto Aida's back, and together they began their adventure.

A JOURNEY THROUGH THE MEADOW

As they traveled through the meadow, Aida moved slowly and carefully, making sure her little friend felt safe. They passed blooming flowers and tall trees, where the colorful birds sang sweet melodies. Along the way, they met other dinosaurs who were amazed to see such an unusual pair—a big Ankylosaurus and a tiny bunny!

"Look at them!" chuckled a group of Triceratops. "What an odd friendship!"

But Aida didn't mind. She knew that friendships come in all shapes and sizes. Benny felt brave riding on Aida's back, and he began to giggle at the sights around him.

A NEW CHALLENGE

Suddenly, they reached a rocky area where the ground was uneven and covered in sharp stones. Aida stopped and frowned.

"Oh dear, I can't walk over this. It's too rough for my legs."

Benny looked worried. "How will we get past?"

Aida thought for a moment and said, "We have to be clever! Can you hop across the stones and find a safe path for me?"

Benny took a deep breath, his little heart pounding, and began to hop carefully from rock to rock. Aida watched proudly as he zigzagged through the sharp stones, making sure to find a clear route. After a little while, Benny found a safe path and came back to Aida.

"It's all clear! Follow me!" Benny called excitedly.

HOME AT LAST

With Benny's guidance, Aida carefully maneuvered over the rocks, grateful for her small friend's bravery. Soon enough, they reached a beautiful patch of grass where

Benny's family lived. The little bunny's eyes sparkled with joy.

"Thank you, Aida!" he squeaked, hopping up and down. "You're the best friend I could ever have!"

Aida smiled, her heart swelling with happiness. "And you are mine, Benny! I'm so glad we found each other."

THE MORAL OF THE STORY

From that day on, Aida and Benny became the best of friends. They learned that true friendship doesn't depend on size or strength; it's about being there for each other, no matter the challenge.

So remember, little ones: friendships can blossom in the most unexpected places, and every creature, big or small, has something special to offer.

The Pterodactyl Who Was Afraid to Fly

THE LAND OF DINOSAURS

In a time long ago, in a land filled with towering mountains, vibrant forests, and flowing rivers, lived an amazing assortment of creatures - the dinosaurs. Among these magnificent beings were the graceful Pterodactyls, who soared effortlessly across the sky like dancing leaves in the wind. They had wings that could stretch wide, and with a little flap, they could glide over their land.

MEET LILA

One of these Pterodactyls was a little one named Lila. Lila had the prettiest blue wings with tiny white dots that shimmered like stars. However, unlike the other Pterodactyls, Lila had a secret. She was afraid of flying. Whenever the gentle breeze would pick up, and her friends started flapping their wings to take off, Lila would feel a fluttering in her belly that was not the nice kind.

Lila preferred to stay close to the ground, where flowers bloomed and bugs hopped. She would watch her friends swoop and glide, sometimes even looping around the clouds, and feeling a mix of awe and worry. What if she couldn't do it? What if she fell?

ENCOURAGEMENT FROM FRIENDS

Lila's best friend, a cheerful, bright-green Pterodactyl named Toby, noticed her unhappiness. One sunny morning, Toby hopped over to Lila and said, "Hey, Lila, let's play with the clouds today! It's lots of fun up there!"

Lila sighed but shook her head. "I dunno, Toby. What if I fall?"

Toby gave her a warm smile. "It's okay, Lila. If you fall, you can try again. I had to practice lots of times to fly well."

Then, a wise old Pterodactyl named Grandy, overhearing the conversation, gave her a nod and said, "Remember, young one, everyone learns at their own pace. What's important is to keep trying."

THE WISHFUL NIGHT

One evening, as the sky was colored with the prettiest shades of orange and purple, Lila sat on her favorite rock watching the sunset. As stars began to twinkle in the sky, Lila quietly wished upon the first star. "I wish that one day I could fly as high as my friends... without fear."

The stars winked back at her as if they heard her wish, and Lila felt a small spark of hope grow inside her.

THE DAY OF THE BIG LEAP

The next morning was perfect, with the sun shining wide and the sky as blue as her wings. Toby flapped over and said, "Come on, Lila, let's go to the top of Pterodactyl Peak. It's going to be amazing!"

Lila hesitated but remembered her wish. She took a deep breath and nodded. "Okay, Toby, let's do it."

Up, up they climbed until they reached the top of the Peak. Lila peeked down timidly and saw the land spread out like a beautiful quilt made of greens and blues. Her heart raced fast like a little drum.

"Ready when you are!" called Toby, who spread his wings and dived into the sky. Lila stood nervously on her tippy toes. She looked at her wings and whispered, "You can do this."

TAKING THE DIVE

Slowly, she stretched her wings out, feeling the soft air under them. She remembered Grandy's words, the star's twinkle, and Toby's encouragement. Summoning all her courage, Lila took a step and leaped!

The air was cool and embracing, and for a second, Lila's heart leaped faster than her wings. But then, a magical thing happened. Her wings caught the wind, and she didn't fall. She was flying! The ground danced far below her, and the world seemed like a marvelous adventure.

THE JOY OF FLIGHT

Lila's fear turned to wonder as she spiraled higher and higher. She laughed, a sound that was like tinkling bells. Toby, flying alongside her, shouted, "You're doing it, Lila! You're flying!"

On that day, Lila realized that fear was just a dark cloud that could be blown away by the wind of courage. She glided with her friends, feeling as free as the bright birds that shared the sky.

Lila giggled and felt proud. She had flown, and it was the most splendid feeling of all.

THE PTERODACTYL'S GIFT

From that day on, Lila was no longer afraid. She understood that trying something new was always a little scary, but with friends, courage, and a little bit of magic from the stars, anything was possible. And so, Lila the Pterodactyl, with her shimmering wings, flew happily ever after into adventures unknown, knowing she could handle whatever came her way.

And in the land of dinosaurs, she became known as the Pterodactyl Who Conquered Her Fear and Flew with Joy.

Spinosaurus and the Mysterious River

A CURIOUS SPINOSAURUS

Once upon a time, in a lush, green land filled with tall ferns and blooming flowers, there lived a friendly Spinosaurus named Spike. Spike was not just any dinosaur; he was curious and loved to explore the world around him. With his long, spiky sail on his back and a big, toothy smile, he was loved by all the creatures of the forest.

Every day, Spike would wander through the trees, making new friends and sharing laughter with his fellow dinosaurs. He splashed with Pterodactyls by the riverbanks, swam with fish in the sparkling streams, and danced with the nimble little Velociraptors. But one sunny morning, while wandering deeper into the woods than ever before, Spike stumbled upon something magical: a mysterious river.

THE SPARKLING RIVER

This river sparkled like diamonds under the warm sunlight. It twisted and turned, flowing in ways Spike had never seen before. The water glimmered in shades of blue and green, and as Spike approached, he noticed something odd—flowers of every color lined the riverbanks, and they seemed to hum softly, as if they were singing a sweet song.

"What a lovely river!" Spike exclaimed, his eyes wide with wonder. "I wonder where it leads!"

With excitement bubbling inside him, Spike dipped his big toe into the water. To his surprise, the moment his toe touched the surface, the river shimmered, and colorful fish jumped out, creating a rainbow in the air! Spike laughed with joy, and the fish splashed back into the water, making a delightful sound.

THE INVITATION

Suddenly, a gentle voice floated through the air. "Hello, Spinosaurus!" It was a little fairy, her wings sparkling like the river itself. She fluttered down to Spike and landed on a nearby flower.

"Who are you?" asked Spike, his curiosity piqued.

"I am Lily, the River Fairy," she replied with a giggle. "This is the Mysterious River, and it is special. It grants wishes to those who share joy and happiness with others!"

Spike's heart raced with excitement. "Really? What kind of wishes?"

"You can wish for anything that spreads happiness!" Lily smiled, her eyes twinkling like stars.

A WISH FOR FRIENDS

Spike thought long and hard. He loved his friends, and he wanted to share this beautiful river with them. "I wish for all my friends to come here and enjoy the magic of the river!" he declared with a big grin.

Lily clapped her hands, and the river glowed even brighter. "Your wish is granted! Gather your friends!"

Without hesitation, Spike bounded back through the forest, calling out to all his friends. "Come, everyone! I found a magical river!" He roared joyfully, his voice echoing through the trees.

THE MAGICAL GATHERING

Soon, Pterodactyls soared down from the sky, Velociraptors scampered over, and even the gentle Triceratops ambled along. Spike led them all to the shimmering river, and gasps of wonder filled the air as they beheld its beauty.

"Look at the sparkling water!"

exclaimed a Velociraptor, her eyes wide with excitement.

"I can hear the flowers singing!"

chirped a young Pterodactyl, flapping his wings in delight.

Lily the Fairy appeared once again, and with a wave of her tiny hand, she made the fish leap out of the water in colorful arcs.

"Welcome, dear friends! Today, you will experience the magic of the Mysterious River!"

A DAY OF JOY

The friends splashed and played, dancing in the water and chasing the shimmering fish. They picked the beautiful flowers and made crowns to wear, laughing and singing together. Spike felt a warmth in his heart as he watched his friends enjoying themselves.

As the sun began to set, the river glowed with a golden hue, and the flowers' song became more melodic. Lily flew up high, and with a sprinkle of her fairy dust, she created a rainbow across the sky.

"Thank you for sharing your joy, Spike,"

she said, her voice soft and sweet.

"You see, happiness grows when shared with others."

A PROMISE OF FRIENDSHIP

That night, under the glow of the rainbow, Spike and his friends promised to visit the Mysterious River again. They would come back to splash and laugh and share the magic. Spike realized that the true magic was not just in the river, but in the happiness they shared.

From that day on, Spike, Lily, and all the dinosaurs enjoyed many adventures by the Mysterious River, creating memories filled with laughter, joy, and the promise of friendship.

The river became a place where every moment was special, and every adventure brought them closer together. As they sat by the water, they knew that no matter what happened, their bond would remain unbreakable. And so, in their magical world, they lived happily ever after, knowing that sharing happiness could turn the ordinary into the extraordinary.

Parasaurolophus and the Melody of the Forest

ONCE UPON A TIME IN DINO VALLEY

In a lush valley where the sun shone brightly and the rivers sang like melodious lullabies, there was a lively forest known as Dino Valley. This forest was home to many dinosaurs, and among them was a young and playful Parasaurolophus named Penny.

PENNY AND HER SPECIAL GIFT

Penny was unlike any other dinosaur. She had a unique crest on her head that could create beautiful sounds, like the soft notes of a flute. Penny loved to explore the forest, using her crest to play joyful tunes that brought happiness to everyone around her.

AN UNEXPECTED VISITOR

One delightful morning, as Penny wandered through the dappled paths of Dino Valley, she noticed a new visitor. It was a tiny bird with vibrant feathers of blue and gold. The bird flapped its wings quickly, darting from branch to branch, chirping excitedly.

"Hello, little bird!" Penny greeted with a cheerful trill from her crest. "What's your name?"

"I'm Finn," chirped the bird, "and I'm here to learn about the music of this forest!"

THE SONG OF THE FOREST

Penny and Finn quickly became friends. Together, they ventured deeper into Dino Valley, and Finn listened eagerly as Penny played her melodies. Each note she played seemed to awaken different parts of the forest. Flowers bloomed with vivid colors, waterfalls danced down the hills, and the trees swayed gently as if they were waltzing to Penny's tune.

"The forest has its music," Penny explained to Finn. "Every creature has a song to share, and together, we create the melody of Dino Valley."

MEETING NEW FRIENDS

As they journeyed further, they met other dinosaurs who were enchanted by Penny's tunes. Tommy the Triceratops stomped his feet to create a deep, rhythmic beat, while Daisy the Diplodocus swayed her long neck to add a gentle hum to their symphony. Even Spike the Stegosaurus wagged his tail to contribute a jingly percussive sound.

Finn was amazed. "Your forest is a wonderful orchestra!" he tweeted happily.

THE CHALLENGE OF SILENCE

One day, a challenge arose. The wind had stopped blowing, and the river had gone silent. The forest felt still and quiet, almost as if it could no longer hear its heartbeat. Penny's notes floated sadly in the air.

The trees seemed to droop, and even the usually playful streams had lost their sparkle.

The dinosaurs gathered, worried about their silent forest. Penny thought hard. "We need a new song to bring back the melody," she said.

CREATING A NEW MELODY

Penny turned to her friends for help. Tommy drummed his feet; Daisy hummed softly, and Spike shook his tail bells. Finn flapped his wings rapidly, creating a fluttering sound. Penny activated her crest, letting the gentle fluting notes mix with the sounds of her friends.

Slowly, their music filled the valley and lifted the spirits of every creature. The river began to whisper once more, the leaves rustled with joy, and even the sunbeams danced in delight.

THE RETURN OF HARMONY

With a wave of pure, magical music, the forest was once again alive. The creatures, big and small, cheered for Penny and their new song. The trees swayed gently to the rhythm, and the rivers sparkled with renewed joy.

Finn chirped happily, "We did it! We brought back the melody of the forest!"

A FOREVER FRIENDSHIP

From that day on, Penny, Finn, and all their friends explored Dino Valley, creating new songs wherever they went. They learned that the forest didn't need words to talk, for its heart was in its harmonious music.

Penny had taught everyone that with a little creativity and teamwork, they could overcome any challenge and fill their world with happiness.

HAPPILY EVER AFTER

And so, Dino Valley flourished, alive with the vibrant melodies of its creatures. Penny the Parasaurolophus and her wonderful music became a beloved tale, shared with all the young dinosaurs who frolicked in the forest, inspiring them to find their own unique tunes.

Whenever the birds chirped, the rivers flowed, and the wind rustled through the leaves, the forest sang, reminding all of a cheerful Parasaurolophus and her melody.

Little Velociraptor and His Fast Legs

ONCE UPON A TIME IN DINO VALLEY

There lived a small but spirited velociraptor named Rori in the lush and lively land of Dino Valley, where the sun always shone brightly and the rivers glittered like stars. Rori was not like the other dinosaurs who lived in the valley. You see, Rori had an extraordinary gift—his legs were the fastest in all of Dino Valley!

THE FASTEST LEGS IN DINO VALLEY

One sunny morning, as the jungle birds sang their melodious tunes, Rori woke up with a burst of excitement. He looked at his reflection in the crystal-clear river that flowed by his home. "Today," he declared with determination, "I will discover just how fast my legs can take me!"

Rori loved to run. His legs were long and sleek, and they carried him swiftly across the grassy meadows. With each step, he felt the gentle wind brushing through his feathery scales. Rori was so fast that no other dinosaur in Dino Valley could keep up with him. Even the mighty T-Rex gazed with admiration as Rori zoomed by.

RORI'S RACE

One day, Rori's friend, Tess the Triceratops, had an idea. "Rori," she exclaimed with a twinkle in her eye,

"Why don't we race?

It would be so much fun, and everyone in Dino Valley can join in and cheer for us!"

Rori's eyes lit up with excitement. "That's a great idea, Tess! Let's have a big race around the valley!"

So, they spread the word. All the dinosaurs, big and small, gathered at the starting line, eager to watch the race. There were the Brontosaurus brothers, gleefully munching on leaves from tall trees, and Steggy the Stegosaurus, who was wagging his spiky tail in anticipation.

THE BIG DAY

On the day of the race, the valley was buzzing with excitement. Rori and Tess lined up at the starting line, their eyes twinkling with friendly competition.

The Brachiosaurus lifted its long neck high into the sky and gave a loud, "Ready, set, GO!"

And just like that, Rori's legs sprang into action. He dashed forward with Tess by his side. The crowd cheered and roared as they watched the two friends race each other. Rori's legs moved like lightning, speeding over hills and leaping over muddy puddles.

AN UNEXPECTED SURPRISE

As they raced through the valley, Rori noticed a little Ankylosaurus stuck in a thorny bush. The poor dinosaur's eyes were wide with worry. Rori skidded to a halt. "Don't worry, little one," he said kindly, "I'll help you!"

With his nimble claws, Rori carefully pulled the thorns away, freeing the grateful Ankylosaurus. Tess soon caught up and gave Rori an encouraging smile. "You're always so thoughtful, even in a race," she said warmly.

VICTORY IN KINDNESS

With the little Ankylosaurus safe, Rori and Tess continued their race. They ran through sparkling streams, over ancient rocks, and past the cheering crowd. At the finish line, they crossed together, both winners, as the other dinosaurs clapped and stomped their feet in celebration.

Rori's heart swelled with happiness. He realized that it's not always about being the fastest; sometimes, it's about being kind and helping others along the way.

A LESSON LEARNED

The dinosaurs of Dino Valley gathered around Rori and Tess, celebrating not only their race but the true spirit of friendship.

The little Ankylosaurus, who had cheered the loudest, gave Rori a big leafy gift. "Thank you for being my hero today!" he said cheerfully

Rori beamed as he accepted the gift. Through this adventure, he learned that his fast legs were a wonderful gift, but it was his kind heart that truly made him special.

HAPPILY EVER AFTER

And so, in the beautiful Dino Valley, where kindness grows and friends are plenty, Rori the velociraptor and his fast, noble legs became a legend. From that day on, Rori knew that being kind and caring was the best race he'd ever run.

His kindness spread far and wide, inspiring others to race not just for speed, but for the joy of helping one another. With every step, Rori showed that the greatest victories are those that bring people together. And they all lived happily ever after, in a valley filled with laughter, friendship, and love.

Iguanodon and the Dinosaur Festival

ONCE UPON A TIME IN DINO VALLEY

In a lush and sprawling land known as Dino Valley, where the sun shone brightly and the trees whispered tales from long ago, lived a gentle dinosaur named Izzy the Iguanodon. Izzy was a kind-hearted dino with a shimmering green and brown hide and thumb spikes that were more for tickling friends than anything fierce.

THE EXCITEMENT OF THE DINOSAUR FESTIVAL

One fine morning, Izzy awoke to the sound of chirpy birds announcing the arrival of the annual Dinosaur Festival. The news echoed across the valley, and each dinosaur from the tiniest Microraptor to the mighty T. rex felt their hearts flutter with excitement. This festival was the highlight of the year, filled with games, food, and the best part—The Grand Dino Parade.

IZZY'S SPECIAL TALENT

Now, Izzy had a special talent. You see, he could twirl his tail in the most delightful way, creating swirling patterns that sparkled when touched by the sun's rays. This talent brought smiles to everyone in Dino Valley, young and old, and Izzy was known for performing it at the festival every year.

A GIFT TO SHARE

Izzy decided that this year he would create something special—something every dinosaur could admire and enjoy. So, he set off to the flower fields beside the Great River, plucking the brightest blossoms he could find. With the help of his friends, Daisy the Diplodocus and Terry the Pterodactyl, Izzy wove the flowers into a grand cloak.

It was a beautiful, colorful creation that rustled joyfully as he moved.

THE BIG DAY ARRIVES

Finally, the day of the Dinosaur Festival arrived. The valley was bustling with laughter and music. Dinosaurs of all shapes and sizes gathered around the Great Plains, the venue for the festivities. Izzy stepped into the clearing, his floral cloak trailing behind him like a rainbow.

As he joined the others at the festival, Izzy could see the happy faces of his friends, all keenly awaiting his tail-twirling dance. The festival commenced with the customary drumming of Trudi the Triceratops, and soon enough, it was Izzy's turn to perform.

A STORM BREWS

However, just as Izzy began his dance, clouds gathered unexpectedly, and the winds howled louder than T. rex's roar. The flowers on Izzy's cloak began to scatter, and his patterns faded into the gray sky. His heart sank as he watched the once-bright colors being whisked away by the wind.

THE POWER OF FRIENDSHIP

Seeing Izzy's sadness, Daisy and Terry immediately gathered their friends. Together, they collected more flowers, herbs, and even shiny stones. They offered these to Izzy, encouraging him to continue his dance. "We're here with you, Izzy,"

they said, their words full of warmth, emphasizing the unity that lay at the heart of Dino Valley.

With a newfound sense of courage and gratitude, Izzy donned the freshly adorned cloak. This time, the swirling patterns were even more magnificent, and the twinkling stones glistened brightly. Izzy's twirl became the highlight of the festival, filling the air with cheer and joy.

THE MORAL OF THE STORY

As the festival concluded, everyone shared in an unforgettable celebration that echoed with laughter and the warmth of togetherness.

Izzy learned a valuable lesson that day— that true joy stems not from what one can solely create but from what one can create together with the hearts of friends. The sky above sparkled with the promise of future adventures, and the bond of friendship grew stronger with every shared moment.

HAPPILY EVER AFTER

With laughter echoing through the valley, the dinosaurs of Dino Valley returned to their homes. Izzy and his friends knew their bond was as vibrant as the patterns Izzy danced to at the Dinosaur Festival.

Filled with joy, they eagerly awaited their next adventure, knowing every moment together was a new chapter in their story. The magic of their friendship spread through the valley, becoming the heartbeat of Dino Valley.

And they lived happily ever after, with their story retold each year during the grand Festival, making the world brighter one tale at a time. Their laughter continued to echo in Dino Valley, reminding everyone of the power of friendship and joy.

Carnotaurus and the Courage in the Dark

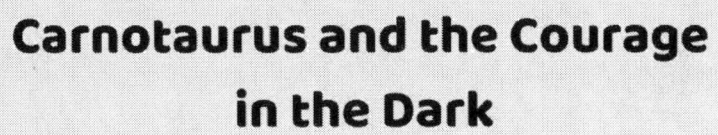

ONCE UPON A TIME IN DINO VALLEY

In a land long ago, nestled amidst towering ferns and whispering willows, lay Dino Valley. It was a place alive with color and song, where dinosaurs big and small roamed freely under the vast, blue sky.

THE CARNIVAL OF COLORS

Once a year, Dino Valley celebrated a special day known as the Carnival of Colors. On this day, all the dinosaurs would gather in the heart of the valley to play games, share stories, and feast on the sweetest berries. As twilight approached, a magical bonfire would be lit, illuminating the night with its gentle glow.

This year, however, something was different. The excitement bubbled in the air, yet there was a tinge of nervousness. For you see, the valley's bravest dinosaur, a young Carnotaurus named Carlo, had a fear known only to his closest friends.

CARLO'S SECRET FEAR

Carlo was admired by all; his tough, scaly skin and mighty roar were the stuff of legends. But Carlo had a secret. Despite his brave heart, he was afraid of the dark. Each night, when the sun would dip below the hills, Carlo's breath would become quick and shallow. He imagined shadows turning into monsters and trees whispering scary tales.

No one knew of Carlo's fear, except for Zara the Stegosaurus and Max the Maiasaura, his best friends. The night of the Carnival of Colors was fast approaching, and Carlo was both excited and anxious.

THE BONFIRE CHALLENGE

As the stars began to twinkle, everyone gathered around the bonfire. It was time for the annual courage contest—an event where dinosaurs of all ages would share brave deeds or face a playful dare.

"Who will take the challenge first?" roared Rex, the wise old Tyrannosaurus rex, his voice echoing through the valley.

Carlo gulped. This was his chance to face his fears, but the thought of standing in the dark alone made his knees quiver.

Max nudged him with an encouraging smile. "Go on, Carlo! You're the bravest dino we know!"

FINDING COURAGE

Carlo took a deep breath and stepped forward. "I... um, I have a story to share," he stammered, his voice barely a whisper.

As he talked, the flickering light of the bonfire danced on his scales, painting him in hues of bravery and hope. Carlo began nervously, speaking of how even the bravest could feel scared at times. He shared tales of his imagined adventures in the dark, the shadows that would turn into friendly trees, and the wind that sang lullabies.

"And," his voice grew stronger, "I've learned that being brave doesn't mean we're never scared. It means facing our fears with a smile, even when they're as big as the night sky!"

LIGHTS OF FRIENDSHIP

The crowd was silent, hanging onto Carlo's every word. Then, as he finished, cheers erupted, echoing through the valley. Red, the Triceratops, beamed with pride. Zara and Max rushed to his side, their eyes shining with admiration.

"Carlo, you're right!" laughed Zara.

"The dark isn't so scary with friends by our side."

Just then, the jungle came alive with tiny lights. Fireflies danced around Carlo, creating a magical canopy of their own. The valley wasn't dark and scary. It was a sea of twinkles and laughter, where friends stood together, dispelling fear with their warmth.

A BRIGHTER TOMORROW

As the Carnival of Colors drew to a close, Carlo realized something important.

Courage wasn't about being the biggest or the loudest; it was about facing one's fears and sharing them with loved ones.

Carlo's bravery inspired the dinosaurs of Dino Valley to embrace their own strengths and support each other. Together, they learned that true courage comes from friendship.

The valley echoed with laughter and joy as everyone realized that facing challenges together made them stronger.

That night, Dino Valley discovered that the strongest armor was the courage within, and that together, they could light up even the darkest of nights. And so, under the guiding light of the moon and stars, they lived happily ever after, knowing that friendship would always guide them home.

Dinosaurs and the Enchanted Rainbow

THE MAGICAL VALLEY

Once upon a time, nestled in a land far, far away, there lay the Magical Valley, a place of wonders where the sun always smiled and the air was fragrant with the scent of blooming flowers. This valley was known for something truly special—an Enchanted Rainbow that stretched across the sky, full of colors more vibrant than anywhere else in the world. But beyond its beauty, the rainbow held a magical power that filled the valley with joy and laughter.

THE DINOSAUR FRIENDS

In this magical land lived three dinosaur friends who roamed the valley together. There was Tully, the tiny Triceratops, who was as brave as he was friendly. With him was Bronto, the gentle Brachiosaurus who was as tall as the trees. Lastly, there was Dino, the dashing T-Rex, who was kind-hearted despite his fierce appearance. They loved to play and explore, especially in the presence of the Enchanted Rainbow that always seemed to shine brighter whenever they were near.

A STORMY DAY

One day, the sky turned gray, and dark clouds gathered over the Magical Valley. The rainbow began to dim as raindrops started to fall. The dinosaur friends huddled together, watching as the once-glorious rainbow started to disappear. The heart of the valley seemed to lose its light, and a hush fell over the land.

Tully, with his small but spirited voice, said, "We must help the rainbow! Without it, our valley will be gloomy."

Bronto nodded, lifting his enormous head. "Yes, but how do we bring back its colors?"

Dino, with a sparkle in his eye, suggested, "We should follow the rain to the end of the rainbow! Maybe the answer lies there."

Excited by the idea, the friends began their journey, determined to bring the rainbow back to life.

THE JOURNEY BEGINS

Gathering their courage, the dinosaur friends set out on an adventure. Together, they trotted through puddles and braved the wind that whistled around them, each step echoing their determination. Tully's tiny steps led the way through narrow paths, Bronto reached high branches to pick fruits to keep them energized, and Dino used his keen vision to clear the path from fallen branches.

THE RIVER OF COLORS

At last, they reached the River of Colors, a beautiful stream said to spring from the rainbow itself. It was here that the friends believed they would find the secret to restoring their beloved rainbow.

As they peered into the river, Tully noticed, "Look! The colors are fading away, just like the rainbow!"

Bronto's gentle voice rumbled, "We must help it shine again."

Dino stomped his tail with determination, "I think I see something at the river's edge!"

THE COURAGEOUS LEAP

They found a shimmering stone sitting quietly by the riverbank. It glowed with hues of blues, greens, and reds. However, it was guarded by a wall of water pouring down from a small waterfall. The friends knew they had to retrieve the stone, but they also knew how challenging it would be. This was the moment they needed courage the most.

Taking a deep breath, it was Tully who stepped forward first, his heart filled with bravery. "I may be small, but I can do it," he said. Using his courage, Tully darted through the tiny spaces between the rocks under the waterfall and nudged the stone away from the water.

With teamwork, Bronto used his long neck to carefully lift the stone, while Dino got ready to catch it as it tumbled towards them. Together, they carried it away from the waterfall safely.

THE RETURN OF THE RAINBOW

With the glowing stone in hand, the friends hurried back to where the rainbow had once shimmered in the sky. Gently, they placed the stone at the base of an enormous rock. Suddenly, the clouds parted, and the sun burst forth, scattering beautiful beams across the valley. The rainbow began to fill with vivid colors once more, spreading its enchanted glow across the land.

The valley seemed to come alive as the colors danced in the sky, filling everyone with hope and excitement. It was as though the very heart of the valley was rejoicing, and the animals could feel the magic in the air.

CELEBRATION OF COURAGE

Cheers of joy filled the Magical Valley as the animals came out to dance and play under the rainbow's brilliant colors. And as for

Tully, Bronto, and Dino, they knew that by working together and being courageous, they could overcome any challenge, no matter how big or small.

Their hearts filled with pride, knowing that their bravery had brought light back to the valley. The magic of the rainbow seemed to touch everyone, reminding them that together, they could achieve anything.

From that day forth, the Enchanted Rainbow stood as a symbol of their friendship and courage, forever brightening the Magical Valley.

HAPPILY EVER AFTER

The dinosaurs played and laughed, and as the sun set, they lay under the shimmering sky, knowing they had each other's strength and bravery to count on forever.

And so, the Magical Valley lived happily ever after, under the protection of their beloved Enchanted Rainbow.

Little T-Rex and the Mysterious Tracks

THE SUNNY MORNING

Once upon a time, in a lush and colorful valley filled with singing birds and sparkling streams, there lived a young Tyrannosaurus Rex named Milo.

Milo was not just any dinosaur; he was a curious little T-Rex with tiny arms, sharp eyes, and a huge heart full of adventure. Every morning, he would wake up to the sun shining through the leaves, eager to explore the wonders of his world.

One sunny morning, while Milo was munching on some sweet berries (his favorite treat!), he noticed something strange near the edge of the forest. Curious as ever, he put down his snack and stomped over to investigate.

THE DISCOVERY

As Milo approached, he found a series of unusual tracks leading into the woods.

The tracks were wide and deep, even bigger than his own strong feet!

"What could have made these?"

He wondered, his bright eyes sparkling with curiosity.

"Maybe a giant dinosaur? Or maybe something even more exciting!"

With a little roar of excitement, Milo decided he must follow the mysterious tracks. "This is going to be an amazing adventure!" he exclaimed, his heart racing with joy.

FOLLOWING THE TRACKS

As Milo followed the tracks deeper into the forest, he saw many wonderful sights. Colorful butterflies danced around him, and he spotted a family of Parasaurolophus munching on leafy plants. "Hello!" Milo called out, "Have you seen any big creatures around here?"

The Parasaurolophus looked up with a friendly smile.

"Hello, Milo! We haven't seen any big creatures today, but we've heard stories of a kind of giant who roams these woods. Maybe the tracks belong to him!"

Milo's excitement grew even bigger. "A kind giant! I must find out more!" he said, thanking the Parasaurolophus family before continuing on the path.

THE ENCOUNTER

After walking for a while, Milo came to a sparkling blue pond.

The tracks ended right at the water's edge, and Milo's heart sank a little.

"Oh no! I've lost the trail," he sighed, feeling a bit disappointed.

But just then, a shadow passed over the water.

Milo looked up — and there, emerging from the trees, was a magnificent dinosaur! It was a huge Brachiosaurus, with a long neck that stretched up to the clouds.

"Hello, little one," the Brachiosaurus said kindly. "What brings you to my pond?"

A NEW FRIEND

"I'm Milo, and I was following these tracks!" he exclaimed, pointing with his tiny arms. "I wanted to see who made them. Was it you?"

The Brachiosaurus chuckled softly. "Yes, those are my tracks! I often come here to drink and nibble on the treetops."

Milo's eyes widened in wonder. "Wow! You're so tall! What's it like to see everything from way up there?"

LEARNING AND SHARING

With a warm smile, the Brachiosaurus bent down and gently lifted Milo onto his broad back.
"From up here, the flowers look like tiny stars, and the river sparkles like a silver ribbon," he said.

"But remember, little Milo, the world looks magical no matter where you stand."

Milo's heart filled with happiness. "Can you show me more about your world?" he asked eagerly.

The Brachiosaurus nodded.

"Of course! Hold on tight!"

Pachi listened carefully, his heart filling with excitement. "Can you show me more about your world?" he asked eagerly.

The Brachiosaurus nodded.

"Of course! Follow me!"

A DAY OF ADVENTURE

Together, they explored the beautiful valley. The Brachiosaurus showed Milo the tallest trees, the sweetest fruits, and secret paths that only the tallest dinosaurs knew. They splashed in the pond, chased dragonflies, and played hide-and-seek among the giant ferns.

Milo laughed and learned so much about his world that he had never noticed before.

As the sun began to set, painting the sky in shades of orange and pink, Milo realized how much he had discovered.

"Thank you for sharing your world with me, my new friend," he said, beaming with happiness.

HOME AGAIN

As they returned to the edge of the forest, Milo felt the magic of the day still sparkling in his heart.

"I can't wait to tell my friends about the kind giant and all the amazing things I learned today!" he said, waving goodbye.

With a heart full of joy and new dreams, little Milo stomped back home, dreaming of many more adventures to come.

Giganotosaurus and the Night Lights

A TALE OF ADVENTURE IN THE ENCHANTED DINO LAND

In a hidden valley filled with lush greenery and towering trees, where the Giganotosaurus roamed and played, there lived a curious little dinosaur named Giggy. Giggy was no ordinary Giganotosaurus; he was filled with questions about the world around him. Every night, after the sun dipped below the mountains and the sky filled with darkness, Giggy would gaze up at the twinkling stars and swirling colors that danced across the heavens.

"What are those bright lights in the sky?" Giggy often wondered aloud, his tiny tail twitching with curiosity.

MEETING ELDERS AT THE DINO GATHERING

One afternoon, as the golden sun lazily descended, Giggy attended the annual Dino Gathering. It was a spectacular event where dinosaurs from far and wide came together, sharing stories and laughter. Among them was the wise old Triceratops, who everyone called Grandpa Tri.

With a heart full of excitement, Giggy approached Grandpa Tri. "Grandpa Tri," he asked eagerly, "what are those sparkling lights that play in the sky every night?"

Grandpa Tri chuckled, his eyes twinkling like the stars themselves. "Ah, the night lights! Those are stars and the magical northern lights that make the sky dance."

THE QUEST FOR SKY SECRETS

Giggy's eyes widened with wonder. "Stars? Northern lights? Can you tell me more?" he pleaded, his youthful voice filled with eagerness.

With a knowing nod, Grandpa Tri shared the tale of the night sky: "Long ago, the stars were placed in the sky by the gentle hand of the Moon Keeper, who wanted everyone to remember they were never alone in the dark. And the northern lights? Those are the Sky

Painter's strokes, coloring the heavens with magic each night."

Giggy's heart fluttered with excitement. "I want to learn more! I want to see how the stars twinkle up close!"

CLIMBING THE GREAT STAR HILL

The very next night, armed with his newfound knowledge, Giggy decided to set out on an adventure to see the stars up close. He made his way to the Great Star Hill, the tallest hill in Dino Land, where he was sure he could touch the stars.

Through the winding trails and whispering bushes, Giggy trotted, his eyes set on the twinkling jewels in the sky. As he climbed higher and higher, the night air grew cooler, and the leaves rustled with the secrets of the night.

AN UNEXPECTED DISCOVERY

Finally, Giggy reached the crest of the hill. He sat there, breathless and in awe, gazing at the vast expanse of sky filled with shimmering stars and swirling lights. But something unexpected lay waiting for Giggy there—a little girl, wide-eyed and curious, holding a glowing stone which pulsed with a soft light.

"Hello!" she said, with a voice as gentle as a dandelion's touch. "I'm Lily. I love coming here to watch the night lights."

Giggy tilted his head, intrigued. "Do you know how the stars twinkle or where the northern lights come from?"

Lily smiled, sharing her observations: "I think the stars are sun-kissed dreams, scattered by the wind to light up the night. And the northern lights feel like wishes painted with magic."

FRIENDSHIP UNDER THE STARS

Sitting side by side, Giggy and Lily shared their stories and dreams, their whispers mingling with the night breeze. They imagined the stars as friendly guides, keeping watch over them and the northern lights as guardians of dreams, spreading wonder and joy across the sky.

As they both soaked in the beauty of the night, Giggy felt a warmth and happiness he hadn't known before—a feeling of friendship, adventure, and the endless possibilities the world held.

A NIGHT TO REMEMBER

When the moon reached its peak, Giggy knew it was time to head home, but his heart was light, filled with the happiness of newfound friendship and the magic of night lights. As he descended the Great Star Hill, he glanced back up at the heavens with a smile.

"You see," he said to Lily, "the world is filled with so many wonders, and I can't wait to learn about them all."

Giggy's heart brimmed with curiosity and the joy of discovery, knowing that with each new night, more adventures and learning awaited him under the twinkling stars and the shimmering northern lights.

Pachycephalosaurus and the Lesson of Patience

THE COLORFUL VALLEY

Once upon a time, a little Pachycephalosaurus named Isla lived in a lush, vibrant valley filled with flowers and butterflies. She had a head as round as a bouncy ball and was covered in bright green and yellow scales that shimmered in the sunlight. Isla loved to explore the valley, chasing after the twinkling butterflies and smelling the sweet flowers.

But, oh dear, Isla had a tiny problem—she was as impatient as a little puppy waiting for its treats! Whenever Isla wanted to do something, she wanted to do it right away. Whether it was reaching the top of the tallest hill or finding the ripest berries, Isla wanted everything instantly.

THE MYSTERIOUS BERRY BUSH

One sunny day, Isla spotted a bush full of the juiciest, plumpest berries she had ever seen. They were bright purple and glistened in the sunlight, making her tummy rumble with excitement. "I want those berries right now!" she thought.

Isla hurried over to the bush, but just as she was about to grab a berry, she saw her friend Terry the Triceratops munching on some leaves nearby. "Oh, Terry! Have you tried those berries? They look so yummy!" she called out.

Terry looked up and smiled. "Yes, Isla! They are delicious, but you must wait a little while longer for them to get even sweeter!"

THE TEMPTATION OF INSTANT GRATIFICATION

Isla didn't want to wait. "Sweet berries? I want them now!" she exclaimed, her impatience bubbling up inside her. Ignoring Terry's advice, she tried to reach for the biggest berry. Stretching her neck as far as it could go, she bumped her head against the thorny branches. "Ouch!" she cried, backing away, rubbing her head with her tiny arms.

Terry chuckled softly. "See? You must be patient, Isla! Waiting will give you sweeter berries." But Isla, determined to have those berries immediately, sighed and stomped her feet.

THE WISE OLD OWL

As Isla sat sulking under the berry bush, she suddenly heard a wise voice from above. "What troubles you, dear Pachycephalosaurus?" It was Ollie, the wise old owl, who lived in the tall oak tree nearby.

"I want the berries! But they're too far to reach, and I don't want to wait," Isla pouted, her eyes glistening with frustration.

Ollie fluffed his feathers and said, "Patience, young one. Good things take time. If you wait a little longer, the berries will become even sweeter and easier to pick."

Isla looked up at Ollie, curiosity sparkling in her eyes. "How do you know?"

Ollie chuckled. "I have seen many things in my life, dear Isla. I have watched seeds grow into mighty trees, flowers bloom in spring, and even the stars twinkle brighter after the moon hides. Patience is the key to the best rewards."

THE CHOICE TO WAIT

Isla pondered Ollie's words. She loved the idea of sweeter berries but struggled to embrace the wait. With a huff, she sat down and decided to give patience a try.

As the sun rose higher in the sky, Isla watched the butterflies dance and listened to the birds sing. She even helped Terry with his leaf munching and played tag with the little critters of the valley. Time seemed to fly by, and before she knew it, the sun began to set, painting the sky with shades of pink and orange.

Isla turned back to the berry bush and gasped! The berries were now bursting with color, gleaming like jewels. She reached up and plucked one. It was the sweetest berry she had ever tasted!

THE SWEET REWARD

Delighted, Isla shared her newfound treasure with Terry and all her friends. They feasted on the juicy berries, laughing and celebrating as the sun dipped behind the hills. "Thank you for teaching me patience!" Isla beamed, her tummy full of sweetness and her heart full of joy.

"Remember, Isla,"

Ollie hooted from the tree, "Sometimes the best things in life are worth waiting for."

With that lesson tucked away in her heart, Isla promised to embrace patience, knowing that good things come to those who wait. And from that day forward, Isla approached every challenge with a steady heart, knowing that good things were always worth the wait.

The Dinosaur Who Didn't Want to Sleep

A BRIGHT AND CHEERFUL MORNING

Once upon a time, in a land where the trees stretched as high as the sky and flowers bloomed in every color imaginable, there lived a little dinosaur named Dippy. Dippy was a bright green Albertozaur with a sturdy body and a heart full of adventure. Every day, he would frolic under the warm sunshine, chasing butterflies and splashing in the crystal-clear river.

But when the sun began to set, painting the sky with hues of pink and orange, Dippy felt a strange flutter in his tummy. You see, Dippy was not like the other dinosaurs. While his friends, the little triceratopses and stegosauruses, would yawn and curl up to sleep, Dippy would shake his head and declare, "I don't want to sleep! I want to play!

THE TWINKLING STARS

As twilight descended and the sun bid farewell, the stars began to twinkle like tiny diamonds scattered across a velvet sky. Dippy watched as the moon rose high, casting a gentle glow over the land. But as the night deepened, the shadows stretched and danced around him, and the soft chirps of crickets filled the air.

Dippy's friends settled into their cozy spots, but the darkness seemed to whisper secrets that made his heart race. "What if something scary comes out?" Dippy thought. He had heard tales of shadowy creatures that roamed the night, and the idea of facing them filled him with fear.

A FRIGHTENING ENCOUNTER

As the stars twinkled brighter, Dippy decided to explore. "I can be brave!" he told himself, puffing out his chest. So, he took a deep breath and wandered away from his friends. The further he went, the darker it became, and the trees seemed to loom over him like giant monsters. Dippy's little heart thumped loudly in his chest.

Suddenly, he heard a rustle behind a bush. His eyes widened. "What's that?" he whispered. A pair of glowing eyes stared back at him, and Dippy's legs felt like jelly. He was ready to run when out popped a little raccoon, its tiny paws clumsily holding a shiny acorn.

Hi there!" squeaked the raccoon, giggling. "I thought you were a monster!"

Dippy blinked, feeling both relief and embarrassment.

"No, I'm just Dippy! I'm afraid of the dark!"

THE POWER OF FRIENDSHIP

The little raccoon tilted its head. "But the dark isn't all bad! Look at the stars! They're so pretty!"

Dippy looked up and saw the stars shimmering like a thousand sparkling jewels. "They do look pretty," he admitted, his fear beginning to fade.

The raccoon smiled. "Let's play! We can play hide and seek in the moonlight!"

Dippy hesitated. What if he got lost? What if the shadows swallowed him up? But the raccoon's cheerful energy was contagious. "Okay! But you have to promise to stay close!"

Together, they played under the watchful gaze of the moon. Dippy laughed and ran, forgetting all about his fears. They danced with shadows, pretending to be giants, and chased the flickering fireflies that lit up the dark like little lanterns.

FINDING COURAGE

As the night grew deeper, Dippy felt something changing within him. The darkness that had once felt so scary now felt warm and full of wonders. He learned that the shadows were just shapes of trees and rocks, and that the moon cast a friendly light on the world.

"See? The night can be fun!" said the raccoon, plopping down on a patch of soft grass. "You just have to look for the good things!"

Dippy beamed, realizing that he had conquered his fears, at least a little. "I guess you're right. The stars and the moon are like friends watching over us!"

A SLEEPY GOODBYE

Eventually, Dippy's eyelids began to droop, and he yawned widely. The little raccoon was right—playing in the dark wasn't scary at all! "I think I'm ready to sleep now," Dippy said, feeling happy and safe.

The raccoon nodded. "Let's go back! Tomorrow, we can explore more!"

Dippy returned to his friends, curling up next to them. As he closed his eyes, he felt the gentle warmth of the moonlight and heard the soft lullaby of the crickets. No longer afraid of the dark, he drifted off into a peaceful sleep, dreaming of all the adventures that awaited him when the sun rose again.

And from that day on, Dippy learned that sometimes, the dark could be a friend, full of sparkles and laughter, if only you dared to embrace it.

Allosaurus and the Quest for the Golden Fossil

THE DINOSAUR KINGDOM

Once upon a time, in a lush and vibrant kingdom filled with towering trees and colorful flowers, there lived a young Allosaurus named Aro. Aro was not just any dinosaur; he was adventurous and curious, with bright green scales that shimmered in the sunlight. He loved to explore, and his favorite place was the Great Valley, where he would meet his friends and listen to their stories about the ancient past.

But there was one story that always captured Aro's imagination—the legend of the Golden Fossil. It was said that the Golden Fossil was hidden deep within the Crystal Cave, and it held magical powers that could grant one wish to whoever found it. Aro dreamt of finding the Golden Fossil and wished for all dinosaurs to live in harmony.

One day, with a heart full of determination, Aro decided it was time to embark on the journey to find the legendary treasure.

THE CALL TO ADVENTURE

One sunny morning, Aro gathered his friends—a clever little Triceratops named Trixie and a playful Pterodactyl named Pete. "Let's go on an adventure!" Aro exclaimed, his eyes sparkling with excitement. "I want to find the Golden Fossil!"

Trixie tilted her head and said, "But the Crystal Cave is far away, and it's filled with tricky paths and puzzles. We'll need to work together!"

Pete flapped his wings enthusiastically. "I'll fly high and look for the cave from above! We can do this!"

With determination in their hearts, the trio set off towards the Crystal Cave, eager to uncover the secrets hidden within.

THE JOURNEY BEGINS

As they traveled through the Great Valley, they faced their first challenge—a wide river that blocked their path. Aro scratched his head, worried. "How will we get across?"

Trixie looked around and spotted a fallen log nearby. "What if we use that log as a bridge?" she suggested.

"Great idea, Trixie!" Aro said. They carefully rolled the log into place, creating a sturdy bridge. One by one, they crossed the river, cheering when they made it safely to the other side.

THE MYSTERIOUS FOREST

After crossing the river, the trio entered the Mysterious Forest. The trees grew tall and twisted, and strange shadows danced among the branches. Suddenly, they heard a rustling noise.

Out popped a friendly little Velociraptor named Vicky. "You're looking for the Golden Fossil, aren't you?" she asked with a grin. "I know a shortcut, but you must solve my riddle first!"

Aro and his friends nodded eagerly. Vicky cleared her throat and recited the riddle:

"I have wings, but I am not a bird. I am bright and colorful, but I am not a flower. Who am I?"

The friends thought hard, and after a moment, Trixie exclaimed, "A butterfly!"

Vicky clapped her hands excitedly. "Correct! Follow me, and I'll show you the way!" She led them through the forest, where vibrant butterflies fluttered around, guiding their path.

THE CRYSTAL CAVE

At last, they arrived at the entrance of the Crystal Cave. The cave sparkled with glimmering crystals, and the air was filled with magic. Aro's heart raced with excitement.

"Be careful," Pete warned as they stepped inside. The cave was dark, but the crystals lit up like stars, casting beautiful colors on the walls. Suddenly, they found themselves standing before a huge stone door with a lock shaped like a dinosaur footprint.

"We need to find the key!" Aro said. "But where?"

Trixie noticed a series of footprints leading deeper into the cave. "Look! If we follow these footprints, we might find the key!"

THE KEY TO THE GOLDEN FOSSIL

They followed the footprints, which twisted and turned, until they reached a small chamber. In the center lay a shimmering key surrounded by sparkling gems.

"This must be it!" Aro shouted with joy. But just as he reached for it, the ground trembled. A giant rock began to roll toward them!

"Run!" Pete cried, flapping his wings. They all darted out of the chamber just in time, the key safely in Aro's grasp. With their hearts racing, they paused to catch their breath, knowing the real adventure was only just beginning.

The key felt heavy in Aro's hand, its power already palpable, and the path ahead seemed even more dangerous than before. But with courage in their hearts, they knew they were ready for whatever challenge awaited them next.

THE WISH GRANTED

Back at the stone door, they inserted the key, and with a loud click, it swung open. Inside, on a pedestal made of glittering crystals, lay the Golden Fossil, glowing brighter than the sun.

Aro could hardly believe his eyes. "Now I can make my wish!" he said, closing his eyes tightly.

"I wish for all dinosaurs to live in harmony, to play and share forever!"

The Golden Fossil shimmered and filled the cave with a warm light. A gentle voice echoed,

"Your wish is granted."

As the light faded, Aro felt a wave of peace wash over him, knowing that his wish had come true. The air in the cave seemed lighter, and outside, the world was filled with an overwhelming sense of unity and joy.

From that moment on, the dinosaurs of the kingdom lived in perfect harmony, their hearts and homes united by the magic of Aro's wish.

THE CELEBRATION

As they stepped outside, they noticed something wonderful—the skies were clearer, the rivers sparkled brighter, and dinosaurs from all around the kingdom gathered to celebrate.

Aro, Trixie, Pete, and Vicky danced together, laughing and enjoying the beauty of their kingdom. From that day on, they knew that with friendship, teamwork, and a little bit of courage, they could overcome any challenge. And so, the legend of the Golden Fossil lived on, reminding all dinosaurs of the magic of kindness and unity.

The Gallimimus and the Great Race

THE ADVENTURES OF DINO VALLEY

In a vibrant land called Dino Valley, where the trees danced and the rivers sang, lived a speedy Gallimimus named Gigi. She had slender legs, bright feathers, and a heart full of dreams. Gigi loved to run more than anything else. One sunny morning, she heard exciting news that made her feathers ruffle with anticipation.

"There will be a great race!" shouted Tilly the Triceratops, her voice echoing through the valley. "All the fastest dinosaurs are invited! The winner will be crowned the 'Speediest Dino'!"

THE RACE PREPARATIONS

Gigi's heart raced faster than her legs could carry her. She wanted to win more than anything! She practiced every day, running through the meadows and over the hills, all while counting her steps. She knew that to win the race, she needed a good plan.

As the day of the race approached, the rules were announced at the Great Gathering Tree:

1. The Starting Line: All racers must start from the Great Rock at dawn.
2. The Track: The route will lead through Dino Valley, across the sparkling river, and around the Great Mountain.
3. The Finish Line: The finish line is marked by the Rainbow Bridge.
4. Fair Play: No cheating allowed! Everyone must run on their legs.
5. Support: Friends can cheer but cannot help during the race.

Gigi listened carefully, her determination growing stronger. "I will follow the rules, and I will run with all my heart!" she vowed.

THE DAY OF THE RACE

Finally, the big day arrived. The sun peeked over the mountains, painting the sky with shades of pink and orange. Gigi stood at the Great Rock, surrounded by her competitors: Timmy the T. rex, speedy like lightning; Lila

the Pterodactyl, who could glide gracefully through the air; and Benny the Brachiosaurus, tall and gentle but not known for speed.

"On your marks, get set, go!"

boomed the announcer, a wise old Stegosaurus named Sage.

With a flap of wings and a thunderous stomp, the race began. Gigi darted forward, her legs a blur. She could hear her friends cheering, "Go, Gigi, go!

THE RACE BEGINS

As they raced through the lush greenery, Timmy quickly took the lead.

"Catch me if you can!" he called, his voice booming over the sound of pounding feet. Gigi focused on her speed, keeping her eyes on the path ahead. She leaped over fallen branches and dodged colorful flowers, feeling the thrill of the wind ruffling her feathers.

But as the race continued, Gigi started to notice something strange. Timmy and Lila were taking shortcuts. Timmy was cutting across the fields, bypassing obstacles, while Lila soared above the trees, skimming over parts of the path. Gigi's feathers ruffled with frustration, but she knew she had to stay true to the rules.

THE GREAT CHALLENGE

When they reached the steep climb toward the Great Mountain, Gigi pushed herself harder. Timmy, trying to save energy, tried to take a shortcut again by jumping over a ravine. Lila was gliding above the mountainside, clearly not following the proper track.

Gigi, however, kept climbing. With every step, her muscles burned, but she knew she couldn't cheat. She was in it to win with honor. "I can do this," she muttered under her breath.

At the top of the mountain, Gigi saw the Rainbow Bridge gleaming in the distance. She felt a renewed sense of determination, knowing that the path ahead was steep and difficult, but she had earned every step.

THE FINAL SPRINT

As Gigi sprinted down the mountain, she caught up to Timmy and Lila. The finish line was in sight, and the crowd cheered loudly for all the racers. But then, the wise Stegosaurus, Sage, called out from the sidelines.

"Timmy, Lila!"

Sage shouted, his voice firm. "You've broken the rules! You cannot bypass the track! You've both been disqualified

Gigi couldn't help but feel a sense of pride in her honesty. With one final burst of speed, she crossed the finish line, her heart full of joy. The crowd erupted into cheers. "Hooray for Gigi! The Speediest Dino!" they roared.

THE VICTORY

Sage placed a shiny crown made of leaves on Gigi's head. "You've shown great speed and a fair spirit," he said.

"You followed the rules, and that makes you a true champion."

Gigi beamed, looking around at her friends, who cheered the loudest. She realized that winning wasn't just about speed—it was about doing things the right way.

A CELEBRATION OF FRIENDSHIP

As everyone gathered around, Gigi remembered her friends.

"Let's celebrate together!" she said, inviting Timmy, Lila, and Benny to join her. Even though they had made mistakes, Gigi believed in second chances. They shared berries and laughter, realizing that winning was fun, but the real prize was doing things with honesty and kindness.

The Dino Who Couldn't Roar

THE MAGICAL WORLD OF DINOSAURS

In a lush and vibrant place called Dino Valley, where trees danced with the wind and flowers sang sweet melodies, lived a little dinosaur named Daisy. Daisy was a delightful little dino with sparkling green scales and a long, swishy tail that swayed like a feather in the breeze. However, Daisy had one small problem—she couldn't roar like the other dinosaurs.

THE ROARING CONTEST

Every year, the dinosaurs of Dino Valley held a grand Roaring Contest. All the dinosaurs would gather at the Great Dino Rock to show off their roaring skills. The biggest and loudest roars would win shiny medals and a chance to lead the annual Dino Parade! Daisy watched her friends practice their roars, which echoed through the valley like thunder. But when it was her turn, she opened her mouth, and all that came out was a tiny squeak.

"Oh no," she sighed. "I wish I could roar like them."

THE ENCOURAGEMENT OF FRIENDS

Daisy's best friends, Tilly the Triceratops and Benny the Brachiosaurus, noticed her sadness. They waddled over to comfort her.

"Don't worry, Daisy! You may not roar, but you can still be part of the contest!" Tilly encouraged, nudging her gently.

"Yeah!" Benny chimed in, his long neck towering over Daisy. "You have a great sense of rhythm! Why not try something different?"

Daisy looked at them with wide, hopeful eyes. "But what can I do?"

THE WHIMSICAL IDEA

After a moment of thought, Tilly exclaimed, "You can make music with your tail! It's special, just like you!"

Daisy's heart fluttered. She had never thought about using her tail that way. "You think it could work?"

"Of course!" Benny assured her. "And we'll help you practice!"

That day, they set out to create a wonderful rhythm. Tilly tapped her horns on the rocks while Benny thumped his feet on the ground. Daisy swished her tail back and forth, creating a soft, melodic sound. The trio laughed and danced, enjoying every moment as they made music together.

THE BIG DAY

When the day of the Roaring Contest arrived, excitement buzzed through the valley. The sun shone brightly, casting golden rays upon the gathering dinosaurs. Daisy's heart raced with nervousness and excitement. She saw her friends standing tall, ready to show off their powerful roars.

As the contest began, each dinosaur took their turn. Roars filled the air, echoing across the valley. Daisy felt a little droop in her spirit; she wished she could roar, too. But as her friends cheered her on, she remembered the rhythm they had created.

A UNIQUE PERFORMANCE

Finally, it was Daisy's turn. With shaky legs, she stepped up to the stage, her heart pounding like a drum. The other dinosaurs stared curiously.

Daisy took a deep breath, feeling the support of her friends around her.

"Okay, here goes!" she thought.

With a swish of her tail, Daisy began to create music! Thump, thump, swish! The rhythmic sounds danced through the air, and soon the audience began to sway to her melody. Tilly and Benny joined in, tapping their feet and creating a beat that made everyone smile.

Daisy felt a warm glow inside her. She realized she didn't need to roar to be special. Her music made everyone happy, and they were cheering for her, not for a roar, but for the joy she brought!

THE MAGIC OF ACCEPTANCE

When Daisy finished her performance, the crowd erupted in applause. They loved her creativity and how she had shown that everyone can be unique in their way. The judges smiled and awarded Daisy a special medal for her remarkable rhythm and spirit.

As she wore her shiny medal, Daisy beamed with pride. She felt the warmth of acceptance wash over her. In that moment, Daisy realized that being true to herself was the greatest achievement of all. Surrounded by friends and fans, she knew that her uniqueness was her greatest gift.

LESSONS LEARNED

Daisy's story spread through Dino Valley, teaching everyone that it's okay to be different. With a little patience and encouragement from friends, we can embrace our uniqueness and find joy in what makes us special.

Soon, other dinosaurs began to share their talents, big and small, inspired by Daisy's example. Together, they created a symphony of sounds, each contributing their voice to the melody of Dino Valley.

A HAPPY ENDING

And if you ever wander into Dino Valley, you might just hear a delightful tune floating through the trees—a tune created by a little dinosaur who didn't roar, but instead, brought joy to everyone around her with her beautiful rhythm.

The music would remind you that even the smallest voice can make the biggest impact.

And they all lived happily ever after, celebrating their differences and their friendships.

The Pteranodon and the Journey to the Sky Kingdom

A DREAM TAKES FLIGHT

In a lush, green valley filled with vibrant flowers and tall trees, there lived a young Pteranodon named Polly. With her bright yellow wings and a beak that sparkled like the sun, Polly often dreamed of soaring high above the clouds. While her friends were content playing in the meadows, Polly looked up at the sky and imagined a world filled with magic— the Sky Kingdom.

"Up there," she would say, pointing with her tiny wing.

"That's where dreams come true! I want to see it all!"

Polly's friends, the playful little dinosaurs, would giggle and flap their arms.

"You're just a dreamer, Polly!" they would tease. But Polly didn't mind. Her heart fluttered with excitement at the thought of flying to the Sky Kingdom and discovering the wonders that awaited her.

A MYSTERIOUS INVITATION

One sunny morning, as Polly practiced flapping her wings, a shimmering cloud floated down from the sky. It sparkled like a million tiny stars. Polly tilted her head in wonder as the cloud transformed into a gentle breeze that whispered her name.

"Polly, Polly," it sang, "

If you wish to see the Sky Kingdom, come follow the wind!"

With her heart racing, Polly spread her wings wide. "I will!" she called out. She took off into the sky, the breeze guiding her as she soared higher and higher, leaving the valley behind.

As she flew, Polly saw beautiful rainbows, fluffy white clouds, and even a few twinkling stars peeking out in the daylight. The world below looked smaller and smaller, and her excitement grew. "This is amazing!" she chirped.

THE SKY KINGDOM AWAITS

After a delightful journey filled with twists and turns, Polly landed on a soft, fluffy cloud that glimmered like sugar. Before her stood a magnificent castle made of sparkling crystal and bright colors. Towers reached up to the sky, and beautiful music filled the air.

"Welcome, Polly!" chimed a friendly voice. It was a wise old owl with feathers that shimmered like silver.

"Who are you?" asked Polly, her eyes wide with wonder.

"I am Olwen, the Keeper of Dreams," said the owl. "You've traveled far to reach the Sky Kingdom, where dreams come true. Here, anything is possible!"

Polly couldn't believe her ears. "Can I make my dreams come true?" she asked, her heart racing.

"Of course!" Olwen replied. "But remember, dreams require courage and a sprinkle of adventure."

THE ADVENTURE BEGINS

Excited, Polly followed Olwen through the grand castle, where she met other magical creatures—a friendly dragon, a playful fairy, and a wise unicorn. They shared stories of their dreams and adventures.

"Let's go on a quest!"

suggested the dragon, his eyes sparkling with mischief.

"We'll find the Golden Star, which grants wishes to those who truly believe!"

Polly's heart soared.

"I want to help! I believe in dreams!"

With her new friends by her side, Polly embarked on an adventure through shimmering clouds and glowing rainbows. They encountered sparkling waterfalls and danced with shooting stars. Polly's wings felt lighter than ever as she flapped beside her companions, feeling brave and free.

THE GOLDEN STAR

At last, after flying through magical lands and sharing laughter and joy, they reached the top of the highest cloud. There, sitting upon a throne of starlight, was the Golden Star, shining brighter than anything Polly had ever seen.

"Who dares to approach me?" the star asked, its voice echoing like a gentle breeze.

"We've come to make a wish!" Polly exclaimed, her heart pounding.

"What is your wish, dear Pteranodon?"

The Golden Star asked, its light flickering with curiosity.

Polly thought for a moment.

"I wish for everyone to believe in their dreams, just like I do!"

The Golden Star twinkled brightly and granted her wish with a warm glow that enveloped the sky.

"Your wish is granted, brave Polly. Now go back to your valley and share the magic!"

HOMEWARD BOUND

With joy bubbling in her heart, Polly and her friends waved goodbye to the Golden Star and began their journey back to the valley. As they flew, Polly felt a warmth in her wings, knowing her dream had come true.

When she returned, she found her friends waiting for her, their eyes wide with amazement.

"Polly, you're back!" they cheered.

Polly shared her adventures, and she could see the spark of belief in their eyes with every word. They began to flap their arms, dreaming of flying high and reaching the Sky Kingdom, too.

Polly smiled, knowing that her journey had not only fulfilled her dream but had also inspired her friends to believe in their possibilities. Together, they looked up at the sky, ready to chase their dreams, knowing that anything was possible with a little courage and a lot of friendship.

DREAMS COME TRUE

From that day forward, Polly and her friends chased their dreams together. They played pretend, explored new places, and shared stories of bravery and adventure. Polly learned that the magic of the Sky Kingdom lived within them all, as long as they believed.

And so, in a little valley surrounded by flowers and trees, the Pteranodon and her friends discovered that dreams are not just to be dreamed but can come true with a little courage and a sprinkle of adventure. And the sky was no longer just a dream, but a beautiful playground where their imaginations could soar.

THE END

TABLE OF CONTENTS

Printed in Dunstable, United Kingdom

70790674R00078